The Governor of Desire

The
GOVERNOR
of
DESIRE

Poems by Elizabeth Seydel Morgan

Louisiana State University Press

Baton Rouge and London

1993

Manufactured in the United States of America
First printing
02 01 00 99 98 97 96 95 94 93   5 4 3 2 1

Designer: Laura Roubique Gleason
Typeface: Bembo
Typesetter: Precision Typographers, Inc.
Printer and binder: Thomson-Shore, Inc.

Library of Congress Cataloging-in-Publication Data

Morgan, Elizabeth Seydel, 1939–
     The governor of desire : poems / by Elizabeth Seydel Morgan.
        p.   cm.
     ISBN 0-8071-1811-7 (cloth : alk. paper). — ISBN 0-8071-1812-5
   (paper)
   PS3563.0828G68   1993
   811′.54—dc20   92-37785
                                                        CIP

The author offers grateful acknowledgment to the editors of the following publications, in which some of these poems originally appeared: *New Virginia Review* first published "Heart's Core" (1979), "A Summer Lover's Book" (1989), and "Czechoslovakia 1989" (1993); *Plum Review* first published "The Uninvestigated Stanza" and "Enough" (Winter, 1991); *Richmond Quarterly* first published "Bear in Mind" (Spring, 1978), "Walking Woods Creek" (Spring, 1990), and "Loss Without Ceremony" (Winter, 1991); *Shenandoah* first published "The Virginia Capitol," "What Turns the Wheel of Fortune," and "Solon and Sappho as Statues" (Autumn, 1992); *Virginia Quarterly Review* first published "Phonebook in a Motel Drawer" (Spring, 1975). "What Is the Most Elvis Ever Weighed?" first appeared in *Southern Review* (Winter, 1991). "Daphne's Blues" first appeared in *Elvis in Oz* and is reprinted by permission of the University of Virginia Press, copyright 1992.

The author expresses her appreciation for a fellowship from the Virginia Center for the Creative Arts, where this collection was completed.

For
John Rutherford Seydel, my father
and in memory of Jane Reynolds Seydel, my mother

And that which governs me to go about
Doth part his function and is partly blind

—Shakespeare, Sonnet 113

Contents

The Governor of Desire

Ungovernable

Trying to counter it
is pitiful as sandbags—
filling the burlap in heavy rain,
lugging the wet bags to the edges,
shoving them up—
It makes you sigh, it's so useless,
so heavy, so difficult to shore
the meager barricade against this mystery.

Here it comes, gathered from snow fields,
the high and hidden springs, the long rains.
Here it is, ungovernable,
overwhelming the reasoned dams,
those useless lumps.

And of course we knew it all along, that lantern
lit night, our wet work in the dark . . .

It's going to be the talk for years
along the river towns
and if we get out of this alive
the day will come
we'll shake our heads and smile,
our lips shaping the word *survived*
like a kiss.

Heart's Core

It's a difficult nut to crack.

Like splitting the atom,
once done, men and
women in starched coats step back,
afraid of what they'd craved:

> box of unbelievables
> blows its lid—
> energies spew, spiral,
> boil into every corner—
> the yeasty porridge crowds the house.

Prodigal fission! Too much!
Too dangerous to concentrate,
to take deliberate aim
at the heart of a human target.

We settle for charged air
over oceans, fallout
on empty atolls—

> exploding only
> the golden fish,
> blasting unseen fragile valves.

Mother's Side

Red hair, red hair, and that pale skin
that cannot bear six minutes in the sun—
what have I to do with those green eyes,
whiskey-dazed, dream-dimmed, and oh,
the O's initiating names
of the potato poor in America?
What's my connection to Celtic song,
priests of unreason, the scream of wrath
from another room, sensual laughter
somewhere outside in the long night?

I with my big Belgian nose, my hair,
my eyes as dark as the fathers
always gaining or losing ground around them
(Bruges, Ardennes, all of Georgia), always
thinking.

I am tall, I am darkhaired, I take apart myth.
But there are nights beyond reason in August
after even *my* skin has burned, turned red,
when over the hum of the window fan
I hear the owl and the desperate whistle
of his rabbit, the hot breath of cicadas.
I drink long to cool down, to explain away
the other sound burning outside in the dark.

A Summer Lover's Book

I lean my face onto the words he wrote,
smelling ink and pine and sun on skin,
then crack the new book's spine to lay it flat
and now I'm on the tree loft floor

where planks of pine across the forked mimosa
smell like paper, fresh cream vellum,
open, sunwarmed books. The fretty leaves
play up and down the page with light,
shifting fringe of shadow on the words.

"She's up in the mimosa tree," they'd say
those summer days my bones grew long.
"Her nose is always buried in some book."
"Never does a lick," they'd say,
"lazy as they come."

But lazy didn't matter then
as long as I could read and leave Atlanta,
uncurling like a newborn from the cramp
of time and space I was a child in,
the embarrassment of hours inside the house.

Limbs I lay on, subtle motion of the boughs,
urged the friction I could find in print.
With a puff of pink mimosa I could tickle
my warm skin and if the book were new I'd bend
my face into the pungence of its ink

then raise my head and slowly let the focus
come, let the words begin to work in me,
confusing as I always have the source of poetry:
places words have taken me, places where I've been;
touching a real cheekbone, reading in trees.

What Is the Most Elvis Ever Weighed?

I guess I could say the answer begins
the day in our storeroom I took shotgun shells
from their cardboard box and fingered the rough
red paper and round brassy bottoms, rolled
their dual weights in the palm of my hand, then
stood them side by side in the medicine cabinet
of the basement bathroom—that was the heaviest
medicine I could imagine.
Did I know how to crack and load and fire? No.
Did I mean it? I don't know. Did the King
mean to weigh two hundred and sixty?
That's the answer to the quiz on my car radio.

Backstage at the Fox he was so thin
and young he knew no need or need to hide
from sex-sent sixteen year old girls.
He welcomed us unguarded then and Carly
Anne sat on his lap. He laughed
and let his slender fingers dimple her bare arms,
while my hand moved to touch the curve of his guitar
that glittered on the chair beside me.
He opened a Co-cola with his keyring
and offered it around. *I sure am happy*, he said once,
pronouncing *I* the way we did, almost like *awe*.
What's next! said Carly Anne, who planned ahead.
Oh, I don't know, said Elvis. *Let's go see ya'll's folks.*
And so we did, his eyes and ours darkwide and shining,
ready to watch the weighty world come on.

Do You Remember Where You Were?

I Wanna Hold Your Hand smacked a slap
of off-accustomed beat at Three Chopt Road
and Grove. Like Hopkins' wrung-wrought half
beats butting into iambic business, Beatles
stuck it to my radio and my stop-lit ear
drummed oh and no and o and kay. And oh now
it's so old, so memory lane . . .

On Three Chopt Road I knew like news
of assassination this music shoot was a shake-
down crashcourse. Skulls would crack,
this decade'd be no easylistening, this assault
a worldall one. Even beats got bullets then,
blasts from barricades who knows where now,
blood all over everybody's car, *ka-pow,ka-pow,pow.*

Puritans

More weight!
Giles Corey ordered.
The Puritans heaved another grey stone
slab upon his chest—
yet could not press confession.
Before he died, he said again
More weight.

So far from Salem
these brown mountains loom,
her Puritan jury.
Above the sliced-out pass to Aspen
the sodden clouds bear down.
Boulders are moving in
on the narrowing highway.
Their closed car squeezes the air to stones.

Her chest rises to each breath
as she dreams of the face of the stranger,
feels again his strange weight.

Academic Year

You quit smoking, buy a new kind of pen,
believing again that your handwriting
can take on character. You purchase files
and index cards, shiny spiral notebooks,
two planning calendars—
because it's September the first.

When that day is over—
a day without cigarettes,
a day you capped and kept the pen—
while cracking another book
that smells like ink,

you're startled by the image of a woman,
lying naked on her back in the grass,
damp with sweat, with the double
moistures of love. Barely moving
she blows an O of smoke into the heavy air.

You will her away.
She is someone from the summer,
someone from another year,
you cannot bear.

Calculus for a Poetry Student

I add you to the moon,
to its daughter, Shenandoah,
this cupping valley, the moon nights
I sat in the wicker rocking chair
holding my new son
and felt the tug of the sucking
all over my body first
and then focused like a fuse.

And I add you to Linton Hill,
that first boy, his hand held
under the desktop (this minute its
thinness is in my fingers). Eleven,
pretending the forbidden wasn't delicious.

To the tall man I held, trembling with guilt
in the highrising tower, dizzy in his kisses,
I add you—

too young to calculate how
your hunger for words takes me in,
your hunger for life takes in me.

One Trouble with Forgiveness

This is his face in the photograph—
normal as a french fry,
a plain old person grinning for the lens
like every avuncular man in the world.
Even his glasses glint
like a newsprint politician's.

Yet this is a face that could animate mine
with one slow smile. These pictured eyes
would gleam for me and reinvent
my blunted nerve ends.
I craved his hands on me until I needed
absolution more than I needed him.

Time itself is a confessional,
a grate of soothing whispers.
I've sighed to time, *I'm sorry,*
and time and time again my bagged heart
was loosed to lift into the moted light,
to make its way, assuaged, through stains
of glass and out into clear air.

But one trouble with forgiveness
—or any solution easier
than pain—
is the denial of photographs.

As now I look at this picture,
this bland and factual human face,
unmoved. I deny the guilt,
the quickening,
that joy, that lust
when this boy stood in my doorway.

Phonebook in a
Motel Drawer

I looked you up
in this phonebook
to see your name in print.
Here you are:
your first name sheltered
by your last and Maple Road
like paneling, a fireplace,
hot coffee and two mugs.

The seven magic numbers
an incantation
to unhouse you,
to change this plastic rattle
in my hand into your voice.

I'm appalled.
You list your mysteries
for any fool to see.
I will not call.

Laws of Nature

The moment hangs now,
Snapped at the stem
Not by her, not by him.
They claim by weight it left the bough.

It stops in air until they meet
This Friday, then will fall
Into their hands, their mouths; all
Our laws, they'll sigh, are round and sweet.

Anger Villanelle

I've seen the innocent flinching at my meaning—
inside my face I feel the anger pinch.
Why can't I say it's caused by so much leaving?

I meant to say Don't go now, but I'm seeming
to order you to leave and call me bitch.
I see your innocence flinching at my meaning.

The toughest I have ever felt was screaming
Get out of here! The crying later was the catch.
Why can't I say it's caused by so much leaving?

The demon in my head is always scheming
to cut out the very one I want to touch.
(I see your innocence flinching at my meaning.)

No one ever leaves me in my dreaming,
where everyone I love's within my reach.
Awake, I see them flinching at my meaning
that I can't say is caused by too much leaving.

Charlottesville, Indian Summer

It almost felt the same as summer—
blue sky in my open sunroof,
the lake hinting water as soft on naked skin
as when we'd been in it.

No noise, though, as I drove up alone,
and something wrong along the fence line,
a dark ring in this corner of the pasture,
a heaviness about the leafless oak.

The enormous wing swept black beside
my window, brushed once above me
over the open car roof,
and it seemed much more than seconds
that it closed down my blue day—
before I saw the vultures ranged
around the ribcage in the grass.

That deer—I think she must have been a doe,
small white ribs so delicately curved—
was most likely in the woods with us last June,
her blood pounding too, all her wet and messy
organs full of fear and love of life.

What are they watching now, from branches,
from fence rails? What's left to be seen—
the only part of her they can't consume?
I think they're looking past her, as you
did that last time, when I felt my bones go clean.

Walking Woods Creek

Something is falling above me
like rain
pattering on the poplar leaves.
But I don't hear or see
the pocks of rain
on the smooth pools beside the path,
only a cupped leaf floating
here and there
on the clear reflections of trees.
It couldn't be raining.
The sky is as blue as a pilot light,
the sky overhead and one that's painted
on the surface of water.

Your voice on the wire
could strum frost off leaves—
oh, it was warm as October sun
and I'm still being taught
how rays of light
how waves of sound
can trick us into similes
we almost believe.

Loss Without Ceremony

That hunger in the gut no one cooks for,
comes by to sign for, to cry for, no one comes
to sit up all night on the sofa saying *yes
yes I remember so well, here, you ought to eat—*

this is the most jagged grief,
emptiness unmourned by any rite.

Not the crowded kitchen
where we sat at her mother's wood table
after the service
with her aunt and Tom and her wordless son.
We were, of all things, peeling potatoes
and chopping onions. *A ridiculous recipe*
we sniffled over our knives,
slicing into the sheer layers.

Later the dishes, the running
water, scraping, steam,
the clink and clank and churn,
the balletic action of passing
from one to the other. I bumped
into her son, who smiled. I touched
her husband's wrist. Over his dark
blue suit, he had on a crazy apron.

*Mary Anne can't find a vase
for the lilacs. Can Alec go for ice?
Did somebody bring some bourbon?
I'll go next door to Lola's.*

It isn't any consolation, said someone young
who hadn't lived through loss without a ceremony.

Who hadn't been a man who lost a man he loved in secret.
Or one who from the window watched a moving van back
   out.
Or one who loves a child whose eyes have turned to walls.

All you can do is walk slowly through a stubbled field,
pick some Queen Anne's lace,
listen to the crickets.
And wish you were in a kitchen
polishing silver, washing dishes,
making something with your friends.

April Fool

In the window undiluted blue,
too blue, and effluvium
of plum bough, pink and sticky
glass-encased spun sugar.

Won't we will it back?
This winter that snowed salt
on our bland hearts?

I'll pull the shade
on these silly pastels.
You switch on something rented,
black and white.

What We Did While Mother Died

I washed my hair and stood in the backyard
of my mother's house, my old home.
I bent at the waist and brushed my hair
over my head, brushed it and brushed it
until my scalp hurt in the Georgia July sun.
My wet hair lightened over my eyes, looked
red like hers had been before, turned brown,
dried. This was quick. I squinted
through the hairs into the sun, tricking
the lights into stunts I hadn't pulled
since a little girl bored in the yard
when Mother was planting her garden.

Where are you going this morning?
my father asked. Again I felt like a child,
living at home: my clean straight hair,
my simple cotton shift. I slipped into
sandals. *Not to the hospital . . . yet,* I said.
. . . To the Farmers' Market with Mimi.

I held her plump baby against my breast
while my sister found an outsized cart.
Ceiling fans breezed the long covered market,
mingling the odors of peaches and fish, plum
and earthy potatoes, soil and air and briny
water from barrels crowded with mackerel.
We filled brown bags with butter beans, peas,
tomatoes and just-picked tasseled corn.
Round melons rolled into our arms.
A stout country lady sold her salt-rising
bread, goat cheese and butter and pear preserves.
Two dusty boys offered apple cider
and wagoned our haul to the car.

That afternoon
in the chilled room
with the bottle strung down
to the sheeted figure,
I asked my father
Did she . . . say anything?
Did she . . . eat anything
today?

At Home Here

Even my prison cell was, in a sense, my home.
                                    —Vaclav Havel

The fork toward the door stands for travel.
The palmist told Mother she'd see the world, and more
and Mother glued maps of the world to the wall
of our dining room.

Now I make maps of the round world
out of cracks that surround me.
I'm at home here, reading my life.

A certain crack is familiar as my mother's palm.
It angles up through the barred light like her life line
that branched toward her thumb into the number
of children the gypsy foretold—*two and a half, see,
and the half was little Geena, who didn't, you know*—

And I the deepest, Mother?—that one tucked
into the fold of your cupped hand in your lap?
Or am I the child that split into feathers—
—I would have loved for my name to be *Fern*—
the one whose fine lines iterate in the cobwebs?

Or will I be the one who ran out
between two fingers—like the branch of that crack
that ends at the windowsill?

The rocky James River is out that window, warm
in July it lets me float in my skin among herons.
Or remember a heron, remember its still decision,
and then the act of take-off, of river skim.

Define Space

Space in the brain
between axon and dendrite
is open to possibility
as Michaelangelo left the famous space
between Adam's fingertip and God's.

The same as the empty box
a day makes on a calendar,
the wedge of shadow on the sundial's circle
seems only lack of light, but tells
us what we need to know of time.

Space is not what is not,
nor the object of rockets;
it's the way they get where they're going.
It's the cold blue absence of you
that bristles me into the future.

Space is the lively medium—
that made-up lady we have trouble believing,
who goes into a trance of not-being,
rolls her eyes toward the place
where you could have gone
and asks us all here to hold hands.

Define Time

The cool blues trumpet sweet
and sad, grey and grainy
photographs of a fifties trip,
the Rainbow Room in one turn of a boy's arms
spins above a billion nightlights,
a princess child whirls into the real dream,
the most magic I'd ever conjured: a woman.
Saxophone smoke in the Village and then
so young, so merry, we ride to an island
and lean on the railing amazed at ourselves.
Senses invade the caves of my brain, now
I smell the garbage and orange juice, see
crescents of soot under my nails, steam
of first coffee city dawn, November, '56.
We stay awake for days and nights and kiss
in the corridors and courts of the Plaza,
embrace in our camel's-hair coats
on the platform of Grand Central Station.
I was seventeen, I am seventeen, there is
no such time called seventeen,
there is no such thing as time.

Sunset on Eastern Beaches

In Tuscany we sat for seven evenings
facing west, as the biggest sun we'd ever seen
suffused the sky in hues we hadn't dreamed of
and the fired horizon hushed us into silence.

On a Key West pier we watched the sun go down
as a black man beat a steel drum slowly.
Awed by ritual, we joined in the applause
as the sun's red rim was sucked into the Gulf.

But the last light on eastern beaches
does not command response. Here on Nag's Head
the air is washed. The sand turns gold.
The whitecaps flap like sunbleached flags
and clean cottons we wear down now
from the cottages after our showers.

Calling to one another, carrying babies
and sandals and iced lime drinks, we go down
to the edge of water. Our faces glow with sun
we cannot see. Our children splash in tidal pools,
their sandy bodies shining.

Matthew in Uniform

Nights in the late sixties
after the 6:30 news of the war
I put Matt to bed propped
against pillows
so he could breathe.

He'd sink into his baby chins,
smile at me and fall asleep.
He hardly ever cried.

But he made a noise
in the middle of most nights
that was a mix of gasp and mucus.

I'd bring him to the rocking chair,
his feet kneading my stomach, his chin
bearing on my collarbone.

His breathing would slow
to the rocker's rhythm, my throaty songs—
Baez, Dylan, Saigon Bride,
Where have all the soldiers gone?

And one song of my own that went
*I'd hide Matt in the basement, I'd hide
Matt in the attic, I'd put Matt back
inside me if he had to go to war.*

Now here is Matthew. As Homer sang,
my tall son is standing in the door.
Matthew in uniform, chest full of breath.
His chin juts above the stiff collar.

I wish I could hold him, hide him.
I wish I could hide him from the gleam
of the sun on trumpets, the spangled banners,
the shine of a mother's mongering pride.

The Uninvestigated Stanza

Phrase coined by Helen Vendler in *New York Review of Books*

In Italy stanza means rooms.
But she speaks of poetry, demanding the nerve
it takes a poet to look into the words,
to check and check again the apartments of the poem.

Listen: if it takes a tumbler pressed against the wall,
listen like a gossip or a spy.
Or with your ear where the plumbing meets the floor,
listen for cries. For
if the poem fails to investigate
the rooms next door, the story below,
the scream that sounds like a trapped animal
will become a trapped animal.

A cat, say, and not a child.

The smack of thin bones in a small head
against ceramic tile
will diminish to a cringe
in a corner of the stanza
written off
with words

like, "heard a door slam in the distance . . . "

And if a poem can baffle
the sounds in its building,
something hard can prod into tenderness
while a pillow presses off
the cries
and we can turn up the volume, practice surprise
to greet the investigator knocking now
loud, and louder, at our door.

Sounds That Have Gone
from Our Lives

Listen! you can hear it now—the acoustic
lawn mower from my neighbor's yard:

it sounds like *churr* only as long as she pushes,
mostly short jabs around her trees.

The sound's almost as soft as a carpetsweeper,
bicycle tires in the driveway, the eggbeater

doing its three hundred turns in the batter
in a big yellow pottery bowl, then the clinks

of the hand-washed dishes, the snap of sheets
and drying shirts flapping in the wind,

the firewood mounting slowly to the rasp
and re-rasp of the handheld saw.

Women pumping silent Singer treadles,
Women fanning cardboard scenes of Jesus,

quietly sewed the seams and cooled the church.
Once things went without us they got loud

and covered over snores and slaps and prayers,
cries of pain and quiet sobbing on the stairs.

Bear in Mind

Bear in mind the tricky gifts,
the ragged standards,
the bad news.

It takes more than one to bear
the pillowed queen,
the fat white hunter,
the exploded soldier.

To bear a child
the mind wills pain,
urges the body's tearing push:
bear down, bear down.

We can't bear to look
at the x-rays,
the black shadow shredding
her delicate cells.

Give us our bearings!
We lose our way
when the bear-stars shift,
the little steel balls
that mesh the mind
spin out crazily,
tear holes in the fabric of maps.

Bear in mind . . .

But what if the mind's web
is insubstantial as the camper's netting,
entraps like a sleeping bag
when the towering nightmare
blacks out the stars,

bends to rake into strips
the woven canvas, the flesh?

In Yellowstone only
scraps of cloth
and strands of her hair were found.

Severe Fire Weather

Warning from the Virginia Forestry Service

It is the weather she wakes to
and walks in now, her body's drought,
fires on the mountains devouring softly,
swiftly, inch by inch, the crisp
ghosts of last month's leaves
fallen from a blazing all their own,
like a woman almost fifty,
disconnected, light enough
to float, but only down,
a lovely fluttering downward motion
to lie, to wait the changes
under the snow.

But then his starched white shirt,
how it feels crisp, but soft too
under her hands, over his flesh,
his long broad back,
how his mouth covers her dry lips,
and heartbeats, breath, desire
sound like something surrounding her
all this fall, something moving
inch by inch in severe fire weather.

Intimate Cars

It was like dancing in public
after making love in secret
the way our cars moved in traffic

in and out of interstate lanes,
now side by side, now me behind, now
you. Then separated by a van,

now out of sight, but feeling the other,
the public coolness of the maneuver
to finesse what's come between two lovers

as on a teeming dance floor, much
of the time we dance apart to feel
the lure of the coming back to touch.

For nothing's more fun than pretending
to be lost in hide and found in seek,
to expect for just a game some happy ending.

Follow me, you'd said, watching
me slide the gas nozzle in. I clicked
the trigger and leaned to see the notching

numbers whirr incantatory magic—
gallons and dollars and symbols and numbers—
then I followed you, into the traffic.

Daphne's Blues

Apollo saw her hunting, "her hair in wild disarray. . . . Apollo thought, 'What would she look like properly dressed and with her hair nicely arranged?' The idea made the fire that was devouring his heart blaze up even more fiercely."
—Edith Hamilton, from Ovid

Didn't you hear him Daddy
Hear him say
Didn't you hear him Daddy
What he'd say—

She's a fine lookin woman
but she'd look finer *my* way

You taught me how to hunt Daddy
and leave alone my hair
and wear these boy clothes
Apollo couldn't bear—

Didn't you hear me Daddy
Hear me say
Didn't you hear me Daddy
Hear me say

Daddy Daddy I just want to be free
Daddy oh Daddy just let me be

And you were glad I didn't love him
'cause now you had your tree
Now you've got your river and your tree
Yeah, Daddy, you both got your laurel tree.

Daphne's Dream

He came to me, the walker from the river,
singing a song of water, water.
He put his cheek against my dry bark
and watered me with his tears.

Singing a song of water, water
he held my hard body
and watered me with his tears.
I could not speak except in leaves.

He held my hard body
As his song of water seeped inside me.
I could not speak except in leaves
I brushed against his arms and hands.

As his song of water seeped inside me
something trembled, something stirred.
I brushed against his arms and hands
to tell him with my tongues of laurel.

Something trembled, something stirred,
my numb roots began to course
to tell him with my tongues of laurel.
He heard my voice say *I am Daphne.*

My numb roots began to course,
Hardwood rings began to alter
He heard my voice say *I am Daphne.*
He said, *I am your father.*

Hardwood rings began to alter,
He came to me, the walker of the river
He said *I am your father*
and put his cheek against my skin.

All Legendary Quests

A dance of goldfinches led through a gate:
I followed from the meadow's edge
and found all legendary quests are true,
the way much longer than I'd ever guessed.

I followed from the meadow's edge
on a graveled path to a mirrored lake.
The way much longer than I'd ever guessed,
I hadn't planned or packed for night.

On a graveled path to a mirrored lake
a crunch of footsteps echoed mine.
I hadn't planned or packed for night
nor had I brought a weapon.

A crunch of footsteps echoed mine,
gaining on me. I had no strength to run
nor had I brought a weapon.
My only hope dissolving into darkness

gaining on me, I had no strength to run.
I lay down beneath the hemlock tree,
my only hope dissolving into darkness
thick with threats of empty endings.

I lay down beneath the hemlock tree.
I'd lain there for two thousand nights
thick with threats of empty endings,
my will to wait put to the test.

I'd lain there for two thousand nights
when the last dark night bloomed into you.
My will to wait put to the test,
now in my arms I held the shining boon.

When the last dark night bloomed into you
a dance of goldfinches led through a gate.
Now in my arms I held the shining boon
and found all legendary quests are true.

Enough

Beige remains of the garden
match the calico cat balanced
on the gate post; luscious shades enough
when the eyes can see
a curve of pumpkin rind, white knots
of carrot lace, blackened cabbages.
It's enough to see the calico cat alone.

The sedge by Woods Creek catches
silverseed, and the mottled windfall
apple burst cold in my mouth.
At a middle hour in afternoon
the stone wall warms, the cat moves.

At the laundromat, the old man
stutters "Honey," strums the lattice
of his laundry basket, grins.
The pimpled student hums
and folds his warm blue clothes.

But the ordinarily beautiful,
sunset here behind the edge of mountains,
becomes too keen
since I was struck by love.

What I need now are things both rough
and lovely, stumps with stone pots on them,
scraps of quilting fabric, scruffy heather.
This lopsided midmonth moon—enough
to see by.

First Words

Could Adam and Eve have felt better
or their new world wetter
naming the black and white cows
in the warm April rain?
Cows up to their ankles in rich inches
of loam, cows in the shed, the clear
tubes coursing with milk, cows
in the chutes, mud puddles dolloped
and steamed with green droppings.
They would not have been naming
the loaded spreader brimmed with manure
or its huge metal tractor glazed
green as the glossy new grass.
But this juicy feeling between us
this misty, milky afternoon,
they'd have a name for.

The Place You Left

I'm leaning again in my doorway
here in the sun that is merely the place
where the sun used to be.

The silence is surfaced by usual noise—
woodpecker in Ollie's pasture,
the Norfolk & Southern's morning clatter.

The emptiness is spotted with objects
you will remember: dome of blue sky,
fat bees, pink rock holding open the door.

There are still some things to touch—
a sculpted egg, thistle pods, my cheek
against my fingertips.

Instead of dog, walnut, lemon,
there's more lilac now.
But even that sweetness is just a place
where lilac used to be.

Branches

Somewhere in here it's there, in a tributary
of circuitry, among the jungled arbors,
the ramifications of the heart—
it's the forked road up the mountain
it's the dirt road to the left
and then
way back in the pale light of April
against dark and leafless hardwood branches
the dogwood flashes white
shines briefly like your eyes
on me when I looked up the night
of the lightning
my darkened room
the doorway open to the light show
clicking and branching its quick veins
into the silhouettes of limbs
of trees attracting lightning
to the ground until one cracked
and fell for you to saw its branch
into a seat that swings now
back and forth
from this bough in my mind
somewhere in here among the jungled arbors
decked with your imagery like intricate mosses
and myriad gifts of bower birds.

Do You or I or Anyone Know

What is this way of gods: how they go?
Down, down below the ground, into the world
our old stories try to show
where life is detained for winter, or forever,
down a god will go
before you know it. Or up, ascension,
into emblazoned clouds, into spun dust.

Our arts, those scraps of history's yardage,
report vanishings
though no one actually sees which way gods go.

No, what the woman sees is almost the same
in all the stories: a handful of feathers,
a dust of gold, a tree trunk or stone rolled
back from the only way out. The strange baby
she will never explain.

Political Science

The Governor studies history
to learn and rehearse the theory
of branching. He needs to know
the this-or-that, the here-or-there
that took the flow to where we are,
so he can say the terrible yes or no
to time. But now he knows
he needs to hold them both
in level hands.

That's why the Governor's so ambiguous.
She says, "Governor would you care
for beer or tea?" He smiles at her
enough to shake her poet's heart,
says, "I'd love to take a drink with you."
She understands this art that leaders make.
There is no other art.

The Governor of Georgia

They cruised through the Marshes
of Glynn, down the inland waterway,
around the Golden Isles.
He was interested in development,
but she was pointing out memories
as if they were snowy egrets.

He looked at her with new respect.

> *You must have been rich to remember the hum*
> *of the drawbridge against your fanny,*
> *to know the way through the live-oak tunnels*
> *to the shell-colored castles on Sea Island.*

The Governor of Georgia ordered the motor
slowed as they approached the Cloister Hotel;
her whipped hair fell like the strands of moss
that hang from the heat-molded oaks.

> *Why yes, I was rich here, more than once . . .*

she said, pegging the pace of her words
to available rhythms. The dockside gas fumes
floated like sloe gin in lemonade.
A man in melon colors waited near the hotel
for his son to putt on the lush clipped grass.

> *Rich in initiations, Governor.*
> *Once in the back of a Packard*
> *in a closed four-car garage*
> *a boy taught me to kiss and whispered*
> *"You've got six more years of teenage*
> *coming on."*

> *Oh I can't explain how rich I was,*
> *two girls singing in a yellow convertible,*
> *harmony at a hundred miles an hour.*
> *Gas in the fifties was cheap as a breeze,*

and lives were endless as gas, would never
run out on the ass-tingling drawbridge
or crash on the Frederica curve.

And there was the boy I told could touch
but couldn't look as we passed the milkshake
cup of gin and juice. In the dunes
under stars we didn't consider the poor.
We were the naked young and owned nothing.

The Governor of Georgia seemed to understand.
Throwing the rope to a man on the pier,
he offered his hand as she stepped off the boat.

I never saw the coast when I was a boy,
but I was rich as you by Tallulah Falls,
leaned from a ski into sunset on water
(a slalom I bought with a pint of white lightnin)
and held soft girls in the shadowy boathouse
and clogged on the deck to the banjo's pick.

Who knew then what was meant by a place
in the hollow, a house on the ridge
or that water that made it down here
was so high . . .

She smiled as they followed the path to the ocean,
discussing economics on the Golden Isles.

The Virginia Capitol

She sits on the top of the capitol steps
looking down the lawn, as Jefferson planned,
toward the James.

Though she can't obliterate buildings
that block out Jefferson's view,
sometimes leaning against a column
in late afternoon
she believes she can see
the pink-silvered river
flowing in swatches of office windows.

She shifts her seat so the marble cools
her skin through her thin cotton dress
and she conjures men and boys by the river,
flatboats poled on Kanawah Canal,
the locks that will send them
around the falls of the James.

But after the afternoon's changes of light
each office pulls its shade.
The sloping lawn is filled with figures
peopling Jefferson's symmetry.
By dusk the square is empty as his blueprint.

The crescent moon comes up
with its opposite geometry—white
as the alabaster capitol.
Across the street she sees the steeple
of the church where Lee said prayers.
It points into the cobalt dark.

When the gaslights ignite along the drive,
the Governor comes through one of the doors
and sits beside her, sharing the backrest
of the marble column.

They watch together the sky turn black
around the curve of moon, behind the pointed
steeple. The Governor leans to her and touches
her arm, motions toward the dark.
Look, he whispers, *look at the James—
the bridges are burning; Richmond's on fire.*

The State of Maine

It was hard to resist the State of Maine,
the Governor offering islands like tokens
of his affection.

Get away from the heat, he'd say,
looking into her eyes with this way
he had of luring tourists.

He'd draw up islands with his hands
or trace one's contour on her wrist,
then he'd smile:

> *Think of it! An island*
> *all your own; no one can come*
> *whom you don't choose.*

She succumbed of course
and came with those she chose to Maine.
They traipsed across the rocks
and talked like starlings. Over glittery
mornings they shed their sweaters
in the understated sun.

Nights were brisk, invigorating;
the lovely discovery of Southerners
was the fireplace crackling in July.
Ideas went off in their heads at bedtime.

But sometimes she sat on the dock at night
with her chin on her cold knees
and looked down the Atlantic.
Then she'd feel the waters beneath her skin
move in desire for sultry weather.
She hugged her legs and thought of naked bodies
sprawled on sheets for any available air.

Firelight in Richmond was in globed gaslights hazy yellow in heavy darkness. In August Jefferson's classic capitol would be shuttered against the heat.

Ghost Governor

Governor Winthrop steps down the hall
like a checking father,
lock clicks echoing heel taps
on the random-width oak boards.
He's finding that behind each door
a chick has flown.

He cracks her bedroom door
to caution it's a crime to live alone.
Massachusetts Bay forbade it,
ordered maid or bachelor to abide
with families above reproach.

She tries to hide
beneath the counterpane
but Governor Winthrop hovers
like a warlock, insinuates his
shade beside her bed, whispering
the words he wrote for history:

"The sweetest life" and "safeste"
was "the life most exercised
with tryalls and temptations."

John Winthrop understands
she gave her heart to Jefferson
long ago, but he calls her like a father,
over and over,
whether to keep her safe
or not, she doesn't know.

What Turns the Wheel of Fortune

A thousand people come out of their cottages
to watch the governor pass,
to sigh at his charmed life, his lovely children,
their yellow curls, their blue velvet jackets.

The golden spokes of his carriage wheels
spin so easily they seem to stay still.
And yet he is passing, passing them by
to the music of trumpets and drums.

He's gone, and one woman goes in to her child
who can't breathe through the clotted phlegm
that came from nowhere. Men go back
to the fields to bend again over fruit
their strawboned children never see.
And the woman standing by the linden
will be hanged next week for whispering.

When the day comes the governor hears
something slip underneath—rumors of war,
of outlawed origins, of errors made in love
he thought he'd paid for—
when he hears a little screech and feels
a forward jerk of the wheel he stands on,

he shouldn't look to Heaven or to Fate
or necessarily take on all the blame.
A thousand people in their cottages working
with the basest metals we've been given—
envy, bitterness, a misunderstanding of wheels—
have welded the lever to start things rolling.

Bread and Circus

Chained, then bribed to dumb summaries
of the meagerest tricks of man,
elephants dance in kindergarten conga lines.
The circus makes the large do little things.

Whip cracks raise a ring of stallions to hind legs.
They paw the air for applause and sweets
then race around a hemmed-in space
while acrobats do handsprings on their backs.

Cursed with cuteness, the panda lumbers to a trike,
hugs the handlebars. Black-white minstrel
in her all-in-fun-folks face, she wears nothing
in nature that shows anguish or wild endurance.

Tigers, in order to scare us, are spared
total diminution. Though their fierceness
is whipped up too, they're allowed an edge of threat
like slave prizefighters and blond movie stars.

Bread and circuses, the Roman governors wrote,
are all the governed need to keep them happy. But
not this tent. After we've laughed and clapped

here's the print of what we'd do—
        hold each other's tail, go on all fours,
        grovel, fake ferocious passion—
to get our bread, forget we're trapped.

Solon and Sappho as Statues

Robed in similar linens,
graced by similar gods,
they lived the same years.
They could have met on a street in Greece,
they might have shaken hands a touch too long
until each knew the other felt a yearning
for something that was missing.

It would be nice to find them in a museum
as a couple, like the terra-cotta Etruscan pair
in Rome, who hold each other, lifesize, lively,
smiling atop their own sarcophagus.

But Solon and Sappho were not a couple.
As statues they'd be deified by Phidias,
two human beings perfected in marble,
equally magnificent on a Grecian hill.

A thin strip of Aegean sky—blue
as electricity—comes between
their beautiful bodies.
Though they're made into gods,
the cords of their necks depict
the life of the pulse.
Their marble arms are only a handspan apart—
if his fingers could move just inches,
they'd touch the sculpted veins of her wrist.

Their once-glittered eyes
give the blank stare of impasse
when the passion's gone out
of even the ancient arguments

between art and law,
between the head and the heart, between
a man and a woman.

Czechoslovakia 1989

There was something so lovely about the way
she ducked her head, light brown bangs touching
her eyelashes. When she walked across
the room, we could see she was almost a woman,
her breasts now points under thin jersey,
her hips as narrow as a boy's but beginning to move
like a woman's. She wore a tennis player's skirt
that flipped against her long pale thighs.

Boys and girls, we loved her voice. Shy
as a child she stood beside the rag-tag band
and sang the songs that she and I had written.
Her low notes rose from somewhere lonely
we hadn't known to name. I think now
she turned our words to yearning to be owned.

For soon the boys began their circling in
the parking lot, lowering like stags, clashing
in muffled thuds that underscored the music.
One night I watched the feisty one come in,
stride to the bandstand and circle her wrist
with his fingers. I saw them leave together
before her song was over.

There was another after him, but time
(I heard three years) between them when she sang
for pleasure in little clubs in Prague.
Then I saw her picture in the paper with a man—
this time one hand was on her neck, his other
on her arm. They seemed to smile
but I had learned by then to read the meaning
of shadowed dents on fingered skin.

And since those shadows, all these sunless years.
We're not young now, no. A joke we would have
giggled over in the park, aging ladies acting young.
I hear she's thrown him out and sings as if
she knows what she will do. I'm going to see.

What if she's forgotten, or what if we
have learned a thin-lipped laugh?
Will she remember summer nights the boys
locked horns in parking lots? Will she remember
how she sang the come-and-get-me songs
we didn't know we'd written?

Election

There are passions of nature
not even governors can contain.

Surveying the flattened acres, the quaking
bridge, the rooftops breaking water,
a governor can only declare the area
the one word nobody needs to hear.

By fiat or landslide election
what will happen he can't cause not to—
only hold the impotent microphone
and intone his hope for relief.

Yet would we rejoice if governors were gone?
The regulation of our hearts all gone?
If they confine the rivers,
route them winding and restrained
through the valleys of sunlight and shadow,
who can say it's not good to live
through so many years without flood?

Though it's unleashed water,
wind, sirens and fire
that cause us to stay tuned, to stay awake
for scraps of news, replays of rampage,
interviews with heroes and survivors.

We search their strange faces
looking for a way to last.
And a way to make our hearts beat faster.

We will go on electing you, governors,
while we long for the earth
to shift under our feet,
for the winds to blow down our monotonous days.

We crave disaster. We will need you forever.